Jesus Doesn't Live in Brooklyn

The Story of Metro
and its ministry on the streets of New York

by John Gallagher

Edited by Jaxn Aronnax

Metro Ministries, Inc.
P.O. Box 695 • Brooklyn, NY 11237-0015
(718) 453-3352

<u>Dedication</u>

If this book serves no other purpose, let it be that it reveals men and women who serve God without serving themselves. The world will never fully know of their work, dedication and commitment.

John Gallagher

Preface

Jesus Doesn't Live in Brooklyn is kind of an interesting title for a Christian book.

It's been several years ago as I walked through Bedford-Stuyvesant, visiting my bus route, that I noticed some of New York's famed graffiti. On the side of a little storefront church, somebody had spray-painted the words: "Jesus Doesn't Live in Brooklyn." You can say that phrase reflects hopelessness, lack of faith, or even a distorted theology. But the fact of the matter is, no matter how you analyze it, it illustrates so many people's feelings - both here in the inner city, and in the rest of America.

Through the book, I hope to let you see that Jesus *does* live in Brooklyn - not only theologically, but personally: in the lives of the staff and the people that are a part of Metro Ministries, the children, the teenagers and the adults.

And also let this book be a testimony that if Jesus really is alive - and if He is not limited to the middle-class neighborhoods and suburbs - but if He is introduced to America's underclass, there will be a change. It may not be the kind of change the rest of America has come to expect, because they equate Christianity with their own lifestyle. Christianity in the ghetto may not be the same Christianity that resides in the suburbs, but that's really not bad: because it's not Christianity we're trying to propitiate - it's Jesus.

And I think if He were here today, He very well might live in Brooklyn, because He would be welcome here.

Contents

Chapter 1

A Child Among Them

Bill Wilson may relate so well to the street urchins of Brooklyn because his own heritage is, in many ways, theirs.

The tall, thin, long-haired boyish-looking *man* who pastors thousands of rag-tag youngsters in one of America's most horrifying ghettos -- he is really one of them.

Bill Wilson never really knew his own father. His mother was involved in a fierce fight with alcoholism during Bill's early years. There was a tremendous price to be paid, not only in Bill's life, but in her life during those years -- a price that is still being paid today by what is left of the family. In Bill's own words, they were tough times. "You lived with it, and you go on," he says. But the result in Bill's young life was that he knew little of recognition and affection.

By the time Bill was 14 -- due to several extreme circumstances -- he was, for all practical purposes, alone in the world and a victim of the insecurities that became a very real part of his life. But it was those very insecurities that later in life would motivate him to do things in New York City that -- try as they would -- others had failed to do in the past.

It was at that time in Bill's life that a neighbor saw his immediate need. This man, who happened to be a deacon in a local Full-Gospel church, attracted a lot of attention from the youngsters in the neighborhood because he raced cars. For several days in a row, he had seen Bill sitting on a culvert down the street, so he offered to pay the boy's way to a summer camp.

A loner by nature, Bill found the camp one of the toughest experiences of his life. But one Wednesday night after hearing the Gospel message from the camp evangelist, this 14-year-old walked to the altar alone and knelt in the corner of the auditorium. There he made a decision to serve Christ -- a decision that he still tells in very adamant language, a decision that he has never gone back on and never will.

Back home, although Bill's life had taken a change in direction, he was still faced with reality. It wasn't long after that his father died of a heart-attack, and it seemed that things were going from bad to worse. As Bill's commitment to the Lord grew, he decided it might be better for him to stay at the church -- it seemed the most viable option at that point because of the situation at home. Rev. Wayne and Evelyn Pitts were his pastors, and they opened their home to him. He stayed with them and at the church, working odd jobs as he made his way through high school. Bill readily admits that it was an incredibly difficult time, but there was a new influence at work in his life: the presence of God.

As he grew up, Bill didn't seem positioned for ministry. Rather, he found himself most adept at things mechanical and technical. Eventually he went to work for a Ford agency and tried his hand at race driving.

But when it came down to it, he still knew that God had other plans for him -- plans that involved *him* in the work of the Lord.

So it followed that when he graduated from high school, Bill enrolled in Southeastern Bible College in Lakeland, Florida.

Unfortunately ... he hated it!

Uncomfortable and restless, still fighting the loner attitude, Bill ground through the first year and part of the second year at Southeastern, but because *there was no real direction* or seemingly any reason to stay, he couldn't see the point in pursuing his education. It wasn't until the second semester of the second year -- in a chapel service at the Bible College -- that a message was preached by a guest speaker, exhorting the students to a full-time commitment. Once again, Bill walked a church aisle alone, knelt down in the left-hand comer of the auditorium without fanfare or hoopla, and said, "Lord, if you can use me, then I'll do my best."

That summer, Bill returned to his home church in St. Petersburg, Florida. Bill saw the need to bring children to Vacation Bible School and began following them up with his own concept of neighborhood Bible Clubs. Bill worked to involve the VBS children in the church that summer. He worked part-time, and as he returned to school, he became driven toward more personal effectiveness as a witness for Christ.

Yet no matter what he did, it never seemed to be enough. Finally, still struggling with his restlessness, he began his bout with heart disease, obviously a hereditary problem. It became a source of struggle to the young man. A minor heart-attack actually caused him to collapse in the office one afternoon. And he realized there would be more to this problem than he had imagined. But even today he speaks of the episode with the clear-cut memory of the fear that gripped him that day. But he also remembered his commitment, and he knew that life moves on.

After recovery and graduation, Bill obtained a full-time position at his home church, Suncoast Cathedral in

St. Petersburg, where he structured the largest Sunday School busing operation in his denomination.

After nearly seven years of service at his home church, which came after Wayne Pitts' resignation to the leadership of Rev. Don and Arthelene Rippy -- to whom Bill gives the credit for his ministerial development, the restlessness set in again. By this time, Pastor Tommy Barnett, who had built the largest Assembly of God Sunday School in America, was looking for someone to head up the bus ministry there in Davenport, Iowa. Bill had met Barnett when Barnett was still an evangelist and had visited the home church in St. Petersburg. Feeling he had more to give, Bill went to work with Pastor Barnett in Iowa. Barnett himself, whom Wilson calls a constant source of motivation, set the pace.

Although Bill worked hard to do his best for Barnett and the Davenport church, he was still feeling the restlessness that seemed to constantly plague him. After four years, Bill began commuting back and forth to New York City, knowing there was always more to do, never being satisfied, wondering where he would end up in life. He spent much time helping friends in the "Train Depot" company of Tampa, Florida write Sunday School curriculum.

Whether it was in Florida, whether it was in Iowa, whether it was in ministry or whether it was writing literature, the gnawing restlessness persisted. Bill made himself feel comfortable wherever he was, but still, there was that restlessness ... that longing in his spirit. He still knew this was not the place God intended ultimately for him. This was still not the exact ministry he had been trying to find.

But the day came when that "exact ministry" came to light. And Bill Wilson -- restlessness giving way to keen anticipation -- headed for the concrete jungle called Brooklyn.

He crossed the Verrazano Bridge to view his new parish in 1979. He had little encouragement and no support -- in fact, most of his friends and most of the people who knew the area told Bill to stay away. Churches came and went in New York City like fireflies in an August night, and none of them made a bit of difference in the neighborhoods.

A Las Vegas bookmaker, looking at Bill Wilson with all his earthly possessions in a small U-Haul trailer, would have laughed at the odds for his success.

After all, here was a skinny guy from the hay fields of mid-America ... come to the toughest part of New York to "show" Jesus to a community of people whose only reference to that name was in profanity.

But Bill was not a rube -- no hayseed or greenhorn. He knew what he was getting into. He could not be accused of being naive -- nor the fool rushing in where angels fear to tread. On the contrary, he had the feeling that *angels* were rushing in with *him!* He had been to New York before -- to check out the territory ... to look into the face of poverty, hostility, pain and hunger -- and he came away knowing that this was where God wanted him. He had hunted until he found the area most in need of a solid, Christian outreach -- Brooklyn, one of the most vile hellholes of the United States. This would be the new home of Bill's pioneer outreach: Metro Ministries.

Bill Wilson had come to take on the mean streets of New York -- not alone, but with a silent partner ... Almighty God.

Chapter 2

The ~~Rotten~~ Forgotten Apple

New York City is a horrifying mission field.

A recent report issued by the New York City Department of Health and Mental Hygiene states that the inequality between the "haves" and the "have nots" of the city continues to increase on several dimensions. The gap between immigrants and non-immigrants grew wider on nearly all dimensions of economic and financial well-being, quality of life, and satisfaction. Income and race can literally make the difference between life and death in New York City. Simply put, how much you make, where you live and what your race or ethnicity is, can determine how sick you are. For instance, the life expectancy of those who live in the poorest neighborhoods is eight years shorter than those who live in the wealthiest neighborhoods.

More than 4,000 deaths a year would be prevented if the mortality rate in the poorest neighborhoods was brought down to the level of where the wealthiest live, the report estimated.

Also, in the lowest-income neighborhoods two of every three deaths are premature (before the age of 75), compared with two of every five deaths in the higher-income neighborhoods. And the death rate from AIDS is the highest among African-Americans and people who live in the poorest neighborhoods.

New York City began the New Year of 2004 with the largest numbers of men, women and especially children crowding into its shelters since the city began keeping records 20 years ago. According to the city's Department of Homeless Services, the night of January 2 saw 38,222 homeless people forced to turn to the city's municipal shelter system. Another 1,500 or so beds were filled in churches and private facilities. Out of this total, at least 16,600 were children, 18 and under. They constitute 43 percent of municipal shelter residents and are by far the largest and fastest-growing segment.

Since 1998 the New York City homeless shelter population has increased by 80 percent, from 21,100 people in shelters each night to 37,900 people per night currently.

Over 60 percent of homeless families previously resided in four of New York City's poorest neighborhoods (the South Bronx, Harlem, Bedford-Stuyvesant, and East New York). The average stay for homeless families in the city shelter system has nearly doubled over the past decade, from six months in 1992 to twelve months today.

During a recent five year period, nearly one of every ten black children and one of every twenty Latino children in New York City resided in the homeless shelter system.

One underlying factor with homelessness is the sharp decline in affordable housing. U.S. census figures document a drop in the number of New York City apartments renting for under $500 a month from over one million in 1990 to 491,000 in 2000. A large portion of the units being built in the last decades are far beyond the reach of the average worker. In addition, city and state authorities have been undermining the rent control laws, further pushing rents up.

The NYC Coalition Against Hunger conducted its own survey comparing New York with the 25 other cities in the Conference of Mayors report. It found that there was a 26 percent increase in requests for food from 2002 to 2003 in New York compared with a 17 percent increase in the 25 other major cities. About 50 percent of the feeding agencies had to turn people away.

In 2001, those living in the poorest and wealthiest neighborhoods were more likely than those in other neighborhoods to have new HIV diagnoses in all racial/ethnic groups. Ninety-four percent of elevated blood-lead cases in New York City children are among African Americans, Hispanics, and Asians.

The second highest cause of death among teens is suicide. Half of the alcoholics in the United States are below the age of 25 -- and that rate is much higher in New

York's nastiest boroughs: Brooklyn, the Bronx and Manhattan. Marijuana has passed corn, soybeans and wheat as the biggest cash crop in America -- demand in New York alone is enormous. Kids here begin smoking pot before they're 12, and usually by 15 advance to harder drugs.

We look at the statistics; we hear sociologists talk about the American "underclass." This seems to be the term that's used to describe inner-city residents at this time in the Western culture. The middle-class folks in America become appalled at everything that goes on, but in all sincerity, let's ask ourselves a question: what are the choices? What are the options?

Time and time again when people ask what Bill Wilson is accomplishing in New York, he says, "I'm not so concerned about what our kids become as I'm concerned about what they do not become." In the ghetto -- no matter what ghetto -- options are extremely limited. Either a child is on the streets, or he's not. There is no middle ground to choose from. If there is a way to describe ministry in the ghetto, it would be the provision of an alternative lifestyle. Because if it is not that, it is not ministry at all. When it's life or death and there are no options, it's a little easier to understand why the inner city is like it is.

That's New York.

In dozens of ways, the city is impossible to generalize because there are many New York's -- five boroughs altogether, each with its own president and quasi-government: Manhattan, the Bronx, Brooklyn, Queens and Staten Island. Staten Island largely stays out of the news because -- unlike the other four -- it is generally uncorrupted, mostly residential.

The other four boroughs comprise the great paradoxes, the enormous contradictions, the often confusing jigsaw puzzle that confounds social scientists, political observers, clergy and urbanologists.

In Brooklyn, the complicated "New York situation" is exemplified -- and intensified.

Residents can actually recall the date and the time to the very moment -- when the good, hard-working middle class neighborhoods began turning into the slums they have become. From the race riots of the '60's to a freak accident in the summer of 1977 -- an electrical black-out that kept Brooklyn in the dark for 48 hours.

It was as if a match had been touched to a social powder keg, setting off an explosion of deterioration.

Over 1,000 stores were broken into. Hoards of looters stole food, appliances, televisions and stereos, clothes -- anything that wasn't nailed down was taken. Tons of plate-glass windows shattered into billions of pieces littered the streets. Anyone who felt deprived by not getting his "fair share" took out his anger and frustration with a match or a can of gasoline.

Groups of looters ran wild through the streets, as they broke into the stores and carried away everything they could hold, shouted, "It's Christmas time! It's Christmas time!"

There was never an accurate count of the businesses or homes torched in those two horrific days.

As police tried to stop the riots, cars were overturned and burned. As firemen tried to stop the fires, their trucks were stoned and forced to retreat.

The smoke eventually cleared, but huge sections of Brooklyn were never rebuilt. Rather, many of the burned-out businesses closed down or re-located -- and the shells of those buildings and homes stand today as a permanent memorial to the futility of the neighborhoods.

Soon the homeless, the drug pushers and the criminal elements moved in and claimed large sections of Brooklyn as their own.

Here unemployment is five times the national average. Welfare sustains between 60% and 70% of the population. The crime frequency charts are topped by rape, murder, stealing, drug dealing and car theft.

Last year at Bushwick High School, a classic urban example, there were more dropouts than graduates -- and the authorities admit that most of the graduates could not pass a sixth grade reading test.

About seven of 10 kids born here are illegitimate. Among girls having abortions in Brooklyn, 15 years is the *average age.*

Employees of a local funeral home estimate that 40% of all the funerals in the area involve men under 40, victims of violence and drug abuse. In recent years, more and more are dying of AIDS.

It's no place for kids. But they are here. As a matter of fact, according to the census bureau, there are more kids per ZIP code area in Brooklyn, New York than there are any other place in the United States. They're here, all right.

And they desperately need help.

That must be why God drew Bill Wilson here.

Of course, Metro's own neighborhood is no magically serene oasis. Bushwick is by no means immune from the statistics. It is very much a part and a product of them.

When a thief attempting to escape after vandalizing a church van was blocked by Bill and a church bus driver, a mob of 200 of the criminal's friends converged on the church, and an all-day riot ensued. As the staff barricaded themselves behind steel doors, only heavy police reinforcement prevented arson -- and probably murder. As it was, Bill ended up with three cracked ribs.

On one Sunday School bus route, the body of a decapitated woman was found. Her drug addict husband was arrested. The corpse's head was never located.

Jamal, a nice young boy of 12, had been working with a church staff member, learning to repair buses, and learning a bit about Jesus as the days went on. His dead body was found, shot ... the victim of the cruel city. He had been out visiting other children, inviting them to come to Sunday School.

Twenty feet from the church, two men were killed; one before a staff member's eyes. No one was arrested, and not even the slightest mention of the double murder appeared in the city's newspapers -- it was just another New York day.

On a single day, there were six murders in the 15 square blocks surrounding Metro -- and still, that didn't set any records.

A gunman opened fire on the ministry's crowded street. One round of the powerful magnum 307 missed its intended target and penetrated the church's offices, narrowly missing a church secretary. No one in the office was injured, but the intended victim was felled on the street. The gunman was never arrested.

This is the Bushwick section of Brooklyn -- the urban frontier where Bill Wilson came to hawk the unlikely commodities of love, peace and Jesus Christ.

Chapter 3

Jump Start

It was an implausible dream -- but a dream that would not go away. Brooklyn's Metro Ministries existed only in the heart and head of Bill Wilson in 1980 ... and he realized it would be up to the arms and legs of Bill Wilson to make it a reality.

He got to work at once, making arrangements to use a Spanish Pentecostal church on Menahan Street for Metro's meetings. Bill's program called for services on Saturday a "Saturday Sunday School," so that his young parishoners would not be in the way of regular Sunday services at the shared facility.

His immediate mission field: the people most easily accessible -- the children in dire need of love, attention and wholesome fun. But if he were to reach them, he would need help ... and the best help available was "hanging out" on the streets, in the form of the teens and young adults of Brooklyn.

Doggedly, Bill hit the streets to win over a corps of fellow-laborers -- the modern urban equivalent of Jesus rustling up a gang of disciples to extend His own work. Bill bravely waded into the human marketplace -- witnessing, imploring young people to come and listen to the message of Jesus, someone remarkably like them ... a man who was desperately poor, but who changed the entire world ... and who could change their lives individually.

Response to this strange new preacher-creature was mixed. Some cursed him. Some ignored him. Some were touched by the words of this young minister, this unlikely man of God with long hair, blue jeans and deep penetrating eyes that were both sincere and steadfast. Some accepted his invitation and united with the youth of the Spanish Pentecostal Church.

As plans were made to launch Metro's all-out effort to bring in and evangelize children, these "first wave" teenage disciples were trained in bus ministry, and routes were laid out. Buses, Bill believed, could serve as the tanks and armored cars of the ministry, penetrating Bushwick's treacherous streets, bringing the Gospel witness in, taking the willing children out.

There was no way to buy buses, of course, but they could be rented at reasonable rates, with drivers attached. The young people trained to act as captains. Fliers of announcement and invitation were printed and distributed everywhere children gathered -- at schools, parks, the entrances to projects.

There was some question about the chances for this wild game plan. Would the youngsters of Bushwick -- of all places -- respond to an invitation like this? Or were they already too hard, too cold, too dead to be curious?

No one need have worried. On that first weekend of Metro's "Saturday Sunday School," more than 1,000 children showed up.

It was exhilarating for Bill and his youth team. Now they plunged in to work harder than ever. One crucial goal: to make the Saturday Sunday School a time for the little ones to learn the laughter of joy, in addition to the value of prayer and the thrill of real hope for the future. Laughter and joy were high on his priority list, because he had walked the streets for so many days, seeing firsthand the hopelessness of Bushwick's children ... a joyless existence where forced and nervous laughter was often alcohol - or drug-induced -- or the result of some hideous prank perpetrated on another child or a helpless pet.

Bill vowed instead to offer them joy, a positive lifestyle and Jesus Christ as the answer and the hope. At Metro services, Bill would break the group up into teams and conduct fun-filled contests which would rock the room with laughter -- pie-eating and spaghetti-eating contests, water-balloon-throwing contests, even poverty-level offering-giving challenges.

A spirit of joyful unity reigned -- fraternity and competition without violence. Underlying it all was the theme that the church should be a happy place which celebrates life ... a place where you can get a glimpse of the happiness that is able to fill us through a relationship with a Heavenly Father.

Fun... It was a method Bill had learned over the years -- but nowhere did it work as effectively as with these young people. The children of Brooklyn, perhaps more than any other children in America, had been utterly deprived of clean, healthy fun.

And, of course, after the fun and games, there was music, song, and praise to the Lord, who changes pain into joy. Then Bill would give a straightforward, illustrated Gospel message -- hard-hitting, pulling no punches. Each week many children, who had been so alien to the concept of a loving and just God, came forward to accept Jesus as their personal Lord and Savior.

But the early days were days of struggle, too. In the midst of all this fun and frolic, the Spanish-speaking Pentecostals were none too happy about the deterioration of their facility. The walls and carpets in the sanctuary got dirty. The bathrooms got busted up. And before

Metro's strange urban experiment was seven months old, the little members got themselves evicted.

Attendance had been pushing 1,400, and things had seemed to be going so well ... Now Bill began the search for a new location. Surprisingly, the move was fairly easy: they moved Metro to the facility of a Baptist church just a few blocks away. But problems never seemed to linger very far behind solutions. During one of the enthusiastic services, the children broke the leg of an old pew. Afterward Bill fixed it himself as best he could -- and hoped that no one would test his work as a handyman by sitting in that particular place the following Sunday.

Perhaps inevitably, a hefty Christian lady arrived late on Sunday morning and hurried to an empty seat -- in the pew that Bill had repaired. The weakened leg gave way, the bench tilted, and the lady -- along with the rest of the ladies in the pew -- tumbled into the center aisle. Within a week, Metro was back on the streets.

Now the search became more difficult. Few buildings in the area were viable, because so many had been victimized by what New Yorkers call "landlord lightning" -- arson. But finally a warehouse was located -- not only big enough for the growing congregation of children, but heated, too.

At least that was the landlord's assessment. Unfortunately, when temperatures dipped to 17 degrees outside, it was 17 degrees in the building as well. Bill shook his head; he couldn't bring children there.

The situation seemed totally bleak. There was no more money in the budget -- no leverage with building owners. And no place to bring the children.

The very thought of having to tell the children there would no longer be a Sunday School tormented Bill. It was the most difficult sermon of his ministry. He was taking away from the little ones the only glimmer of hope they had -- a refuge from the savagery of their day-to-day existence. As he delivered the sad news from the hood of a bus, Bill felt like some bad combination of Scrooge, Simon LeGree and the uncaring innkeeper of Bethlehem.

He could not let them down ... he would work harder...he would work harder...he would do something to get Metro going again, even if he had to beg.

Begging, even in the name of Jesus Christ, is exhausting. But Bill Wilson did it. He set out across the continent, speaking in church after church, trying to convince people that even in the harshest ghetto of Brooklyn, young lives could be changed for the Lord.

On a Sunday morning in Leveland, Texas, as Bill sat on the edge of his bed in a motel room, preparing to speak at a local church, he turned on the television set. The touching voice and handsome face of Dr. Robert Schuller appeared, flanked by the beautiful Crystal Cathedral and its glorious choir.

Bill Wilson didn't need this. He was a poor minister who couldn't even afford a heated warehouse. His ministry, for all practical purposes, was dead. But Dr. Schuller was preaching on a Christian's responsibility to God to "hang in there," and it touched a button in Bill Wilson's heart. Courage sprang anew in his heart. Some way, somehow, he would not let the children of Brooklyn be without Jesus. Yes, he was tired ... Yes, it looked impossible. But yes -- he could hang in there.

On that day, Bill Wilson made a decision. Driven by renewed faith -- and with only $98.16 in a checking account -- he decided to buy an ancient brewery in Brooklyn. He had looked at it before. It had been at one time one of the most effective "chop shops" in the city -- a place where stolen cars are taken to be dismantled and redistributed as parts to disreputable auto repair shops at discount prices. Today it was a warehouse, and it was perfect for the Metro ministry. The only problem, of course, was the price tag: $150,000. And Bill would need $25,000 for a down payment on the old building.

A phone call moved him from faith to fact "Bill, God woke me up in the middle of the night," Sister Nell Hibbard of the Gospel Lighthouse Church in Dallas told Bill by long-distance. "You are supposed to be here next Sunday."

A man in need of $25,000 -- and quick -- does what God tells him. A $10,000 offering got them started. The next weekend the missionary to Brooklyn was in Glad Tidings Church in Sherman, Texas, with Pastor Clyde Causey. Their offering for the purchase of the warehouse was $18,000. There were two cash offerings; they amounted to $28,000!

Suddenly, Metro Ministries was alive again. This down payment miracle had jump-started the ministry's dead battery. And it was only the beginning ... the first in a long series of miracles that procured the former Rheingold Brewery as the new home for the church.

The young people -- who had been Metro's arms and legs and bus captains and workers -- returned again with offers of help. And new young people -- who had never darkened the doors of a church -- came, too. They had seen Metro spring up in their neighborhood; they had seen the love and compassion and the fun and the joy. They had seen the *difference* -- and now, collectively, they said that they "didn't want our little brothers and sisters to turn out like us." These were children 15 and 16 years old, tragically addicted to the devil's lifestyle, but hoping to save their little siblings from it. They helped in the only way they could -- handing out fliers and telling children about the Sunday School where fun and joy prevailed.

Buses were rented again; routes were laid out again; fliers of invitation were printed again; ministers and volunteers joined in the work again -- and everybody held their breath to see who would attend Metro's rebirth.

On the first weekend, 2,400 children appeared.

All the work, all the preparation, all the prayer had paid off. The resurrection turned out to be more than twice as grand as the original birthing! As the old brewery became a church, it rang with the laughter and songs of children -- not to mention a new four-letter word that some of these little ones had never heard ... *love!*

The long winter of discontent had given way to the spring of hope, and in the cracks of a Brooklyn sidewalk a flower had bloomed ... a flower that neither the harsh climate of hostility nor the cold winds of violence, drugs, crime and indifference could stamp out.

Every week more children arrived, to become a part of this beautiful, thriving venture.

Today the kids call it the "Yogi Bear Sunday School." Bill had been looking for a symbol that would draw children to Jesus -- a symbol that they would connect to the loving, gentle, fair and happy aspects of life in their joyless society. Of all the cartoon characters that clutter television and comic strips, Yogi seemed the most gentle and understanding.

So when Bill saw a life-sized Yogi Bear costume for sale at Columbia College in South Carolina, he bought it for the kids. It took all the money in his pocket -- not enough -- and a lot of pleading to make up the balance.

In the children's minds Yogi is still the symbol of Metro ... a symbol that says to the children of Brooklyn: Yes, there *is* a place of happiness -- and safety.

Chapter 4

Against the Wind

It had finally appeared as if things were going to be the way they were supposed to be, but Bill had learned that at any given point in life, a wrench can be thrown in to ruin the entire works. In Bible college, they don't teach how to buy buildings, how to deal with real estate people, how to deal with city regulations ... Between gas bills, electric bills, water bills, telephone installation people, "elevator inspectors," and garbage collectors all looking for bribes, Bill found he had secured a building he could not pay for.

The payments were $2,000 a month, and the ministry's only support was Bill beating the bushes (this is still true, although today because of the ministry's reputation, Bill has more opportunity to speak in churches and on interview-format television programs). But in those early days, Bill Wilson and Metro Ministries were unknown entities. And when you're a nobody, nobody cares.

In freezing mid-winter, Bill and his few staff members worked hard refurbishing their dilapidated building warmed only by the fire set in a 55-gallon drum filled with wood -- and often they slept in the same place, huddled by the blaze. It was a lonely and discouraging time, and today Bill admits this was the time he most wanted to quit and go home ...

A church in Oklahoma City gave big gas heaters for the auditorium. A church in Florida donated the carpet --

other folks helped to provide chairs ... But, meantime, the building payments were tougher to make, and it was clear that foreclosure procedures would ensue if the payments could not be made regularly.

Between people donating old junk buses that cost more to fix than what they were worth to insure, and so many people -- and churches -- making promises that were never kept, Metro's chances of survival became slimmer and slimmer. It seemed that many of the churches which pledged support had unrealistic ideas of the type of help that was needed on an urban mission field. What they offered to Bill and his little parishoners seemed simply to be their left-overs.

"I remember when I was growing up the Women's Missionary Council in our church used to bring in sheets and cut them up into strips and roll those strips up into rolls of bandages to be sent overseas to the missionaries," Bill says. "Today, I can just imagine the natives on the mission field unraveling those strips of bandages and saying, 'Gee, if we could sew these all together, we could make a sheet!'" As humorous as it seems, it's an accurate illustration of how we approach the needs of missions in the 20th Century.

"Usually the missionaries get the leftovers -- the left-over buses, the left-over clothes -- because I guess we feel like we're dealing with people who just deserve the leftovers; or that that's all it takes to carry on a mission."

Bill's respect for today's Women's Missionary Councils and ladies' groups across the country has grown by leaps and bounds because of their dedication to the *Annual Christmas Stocking Project.* Ladies take patterns provided by Metro to make the stockings. They sew them with red or green felt, stuff them with suggested treats and mail them to the church in Brooklyn. This guarantees that every one of Metro's children will receive at least one present. For so many children, this is their only present, and the staff thanks God for the women who make it possible.

"They probably don't realize it, but they have been the determining factor of whether a child in the ghetto would have a Christmas or not," Bill says. "Thank God for women who have seen the need as it really is!"

"That's what ministry in the ghetto requires: genuinely concerned people, people who care enough to give more than just the old worn-out jeans from their closet." Wilson says: "We thank God for all the second-hand clothes and donations, but we really rejoice when someone comes for a couple of weeks in the summertime and says, 'I'll pound nails. I'll paint buses. I'll wash floors. I'll clean bathrooms. I'll hand out literature. I'll help you work on a bus route. I'll pray for the services. I'll work with people around the altars. I'll hug some kids. Because I'm willing to give more.' Missions, like life, is not always as we perceive it to be."

It's an old story, but one that illustrates a valid point: driving to work at the charity hospital one day, two nuns ran out of gas. Flustered, they hiked to the nearest service station, but there was no help because they didn't have a gas can.

"You know," one of the sisters said, "I believe there's an old bed pan in the trunk of the car. Could we put some gas in that?"

The gas station manager wasn't happy with the idea, but he wanted to help, so he said he would bend the rules this one time and give them enough gas in the bed pan to get their car started and back to the station. Happy, the two nuns took the funnel he gave them and returned to their car with the bed pan full of gasoline.

On the highway, a pick-up truck cruised by, and the cowboys stared at the nuns, filling their gas tank from a bed pan. "Did you see that?" one of the cowboys demanded.

"I sure did!" the pick-up driver replied. "Now that's what I call faith!"

Of course, the point is that things aren't always as they seem. Bill and the small staff of Metro Ministries found out that ministry in the inner city is not what it seems to be to the rest of the world. Things are not always the way we see them.

Bill and the staff don't live in the suburbs and commute to the ghetto to minister ... They live in the ghetto because they know it is important to see things the way they are in the ghetto -- not the way they wish they were, and not the way somebody 25 years ago said they were or the way someone who lives in the suburbs now says it is.

"The people in the suburbs are our neighbors and friends," Bill says. "And we're their friends, but we've had to earn the right to be heard here. And it hasn't been easy.

"But just as the four lepers said in 2 Kings Chapter 7: 'there's nothing left for us if we go back -- if we go back, we die; if we sit still, we die, if we go forward, the enemy is out there and we'll *probably* die. We felt the same way -- our options were limited, and it seemed like death was imminent. But when you don't know what to do, the best gamble is to go forward, and that's what we had to do."

So they kept working on the building, kept bringing the children -- and Bill kept traveling and begging for help for the little ministry. And they kept running against the wind.

"We've been running against the wind since we first started here," Bill says today. "And I guess we'll be running against the wind 'til the end, because that's the way life is in the ghetto. And when you run against the wind, you have to run as hard as you can."

Chapter 5

Every Which Way But Loose

Ramon Perales is one of Metro's miracles.

He hasn't seen his father in over 3 years. In fact, Ramon doesn't even know where his father is.

Fire gutted his house in 1985. Ramon and his brother, two sisters and mom were put out on the street. Left with no choice, they began a nomadic journey through the slums of New York.

They were forced to share space with another family in a Manhattan shelter -- the same kind of shelter where child pornographers find their innocent victims. It's in these government-run shelters that drug-addicted parents have been known to sell their little ones for a fix or enough money to get one. And the children who are not bartered or abandoned grow up in the company of street gangs, pushers, pimps and prostitutes.

This was Ramon's new environment. This was his home.

But then, against this backdrop of crime, violence, and perversion, there came a ray of light. Ramon received an invitation to attend "Yogi Bear Sunday School" at Metro Ministries.

That simple gesture -- that ordinary little expression of love -- was like a lifeline to Ramon. He eagerly said yes.

Since that time, Ramon has practically taken up residence at Metro. He attends all "Saturday Sunday

School" sessions, Sunday morning worship, a youth service on Tuesday and even Royal Rangers on Wednesday nights.

On a fishing trip with the Royal Ranger group, Ramon was ecstatic. It was only the second time in his life he had been fishing. The last time, he had gone with his father -- before the abandonment.

Ramon is a classic case of the Metro ministry in action. The strategy is not hard to define: just reach out in *every way possible* to the needy children of Brooklyn.

Bill Wilson & Co. accomplish this mission through several programs, not the least of which are the bus transportation ministry, weekly in-home visits, and "Saturday Sunday School" and Sunday worship services.

The bus transportation ministry is the heart of Metro because it allows the children to come to church. Naturally the kids cannot get there on their own, and many cannot rely on the transportation of parents, either.

Saturday after Saturday, tireless Metro Sunday School bus workers arrive in neighborhoods throughout Brooklyn, horns honking and bus captains shouting and calling. The children converge from all corners -- from cramped rundown houses and graffiti-covered apartment buildings anxious to catch the bus for an afternoon of fun, games and the Gospel.

Even more remarkable than the weekly bus invasion are the 20,000 personal visits accomplished every single week of the year by the staff of Metro Ministries. Except in rare cases, every child is visited in his home every week.

These are far more than public relations visits which serve to remind the children about upcoming events and services. They give staffers a chance to meet parents and family, to minister personally, to pray with them, and encourage them to attend services as well.

These crucial visits also allow the staff of Metro Ministries to make sure that each child has adequate living conditions and is receiving the food and clothing he needs to survive. When those conditions are not being met, positive steps can be taken to correct the situation -- hundreds of children and their families have received food, clothing, and other essentials through the do-whatever-it-takes ministry of Metro Ministries.

Concerned adult friends from across New York and across the nation "sponsor" children into the Metro program. For a monthly donation of $23, a needy child can be sure to receive a weekly visit, food and clothing as necessary and transportation to Saturday Sunday School. In return, the sponsor receives a picture and birth date on the child being helped in this way, so they can pray for the child and communicate through the ministry offices.

Of course, at the heart of Metro's ministry are the fun-filled Sunday School services. The often bleak existence of the little ones of Brooklyn is broken for the weekend, as they take in a time of laughter, lightheartedness, singing and happiness.

Metro is a place of love, compassion, friendship and protection from the cruel world ... an alternative to drugs, street violence and crime. Services have grown steadily since Bill Wilson and his teenage helpers made their first brave forays into the Bushwick streets. Today over 20,000 children and young people attend services each week.

Most essential of all: the children absorb the truth of God's love -- that someone, somewhere cares about them! They have the opportunity to receive Christ in exciting weekly Christ-centered classes that offer an alternative to the ways of life that the neighborhood offers and teaches them that they can resist drugs and immorality.

And they have the opportunity to become part of a loving, caring community of believers, dedicated to the kingdom of God, along with new adult role models and Christian friends who can help them build an early foundation for faithfulness and righteousness.

For many children, Metro Ministries is the only real opportunity for peace and freedom they may have!

The next three chapters -- about buses, services and visits -- better explain each of these remarkable, all-important ministries. But these are only the biggest and most visible outreaches. Other ongoing ministries of Metro include:

Feeding the hungry. Providing food items for the kids in Sunday School.

Clothing the poor. Three days a week at Metro, clothes are given to the ragged.

Street Preaching. Metro staffers hit the streets with Sidewalk Sunday School trucks, penetrating the exteriors of Brooklyn. An area is roped off around the truck for the "instant congregation" to gather to listen to music from a Christian band and hear the Word.

Expansion. Not only has New York become a catalyst of outreach and motivation, but it has also become a foundation of resources. Direct off-shoots of the Sunday School have been created in places such as Dallas-Fort-Worth, Buffalo, Tallahassee, Houston and Washington, D.C.. You will find other ministries conceptually patterned after Metro in places like Australia, Scotland, Belfast, the Philippines, Africa and parts of South America.

And new strategies of outreach are being launched practically every month, as the dedicated Bill Wilson and his equally dedicated workers search for new ways to communicate their all-consuming message: "God loves you, and He can transform your life!"

Chapter 6

Chariots of Fire

It is not safe enough for adults to walk through these rugged streets, let alone children. Consequently, buses are essential to maintaining the ministry of the Metro Church, which now stretches into four boroughs. If Metro's workers are invading soldiers in enemy territory, the buses are the tanks.

It is no smooth terrain. Some have said the only thing this community requires more than God's love is a huge construction gang to pave its pock-marked roads. For a staff member to drive a bus here, it takes the agility of a tightrope walker, the courage of a combat veteran on the Burma Road, the automotive skill of an Indy 500 race driver -- and the patience of Job. Prayer also helps.

People don't double-park in Brooklyn -- they triple park. Maneuvering through the clogged avenues is a feat of genius in itself. Tickets are rarely given out to the violators, and arresting non-payers of fines is not a high priority among the harried police.

Some of Metro's buses are 15 years old. Many are hand-me-downs, donations from congregations who could afford better, newer vehicles. It is miraculous that they run let alone pass New York's annual motor vehicle inspection. They are a tribute to the men whose ministry is the screwdriver, the piston and a lug wrench.

Out on the route, bus ministry becomes an on-the-job lesson in diplomacy. This hot June Saturday, a couple of members of a Black Muslim group intentionally try to block the way of a Metro bus at a narrow pass. Bill Wilson is driving -- yes, even at the helm of the sprawling ministry, he still maintains his own bus route and rigorous schedule of home visitations. Now, in the face of the Muslim sneers, he backs up several feet and slowly proceeds forward, trying to squeeze past the barricade. He has been in tighter spots; he makes this one, too. Such scrapes with enemies of the ministry are trying - but commonplace.

As a Metro bus pulls up and stops at a housing project or designated corner, the bus siren goes off like a strange cathedral bell calling the faithful to gather. The children are either waiting impatiently or rushing out of buildings *en masse,* afraid they'll be late. Parents shout good-byes and warnings.

"You be a good boy, Louis - don't you be wrecking that place!"

"Say hello to Jesus for me, Gloria!"

Stop after stop, more and more children crowd the bus - most of them conspicuously neat and clean and well-dressed for their day out. They greet the drivers and bus captains with first names and often with little kisses. The drivers and captains respond in kind - these kids are *their* kids; they know them by name, by background, by every detail of personality.

The children are full of joy and laughter and song, as if they are going on a picnic - no longer the deprived castaways of a blighted neighborhood, but happy tots off to visit with Jesus.

The bus cannot take the scenic route. There is no such thing. The scenery is, as usual, variegated. It also has a way of interacting with the children on the bus. One example: It is customary (although illegal) for people to open the fire hydrants when the temperature rises. Still, as the Metro bus passes, adults in the street are pressuring the openings of hydrants to spray the open-windowed vehicles -- to the delight, laughter and screams of the children. In Dubuque or Boise, this might be considered criminal. In Brooklyn, it is a harmless game.

There is singing and hand-clapping all the way to the church. From bus after overcrowded bus, the children rush out to the church, the fun, the games, and -- most of all -- to Jesus.

Each child's hand is marked with his bus number so he won't get lost. After the service, there is a head count, and the buses roll again to drop the children off. The same happy ritual, the chapel bells of laughter, the singing, and -- on this day -- a surprise ...

Each child receives a big piece of watermelon as he exits the bus. The little ones' eyes are like bowling balls as "bus pastors" assist them off the vehicles so they won't drop their prizes.

Shouts of "Good bye, Bill!" and "Thank you, Gloria!" and blown kisses fill the humid sunlight. Six bus rides and three services later, laughter lingers into the night.

And the big "Christian tanks" finally line up on a parking lot, surrounded by barbed wire, and let off their tired but happy invaders.

Bill Wilson wanted to help a bunch of kids whom no one seemed to care about ... Today he is bringing them the Gospel and love of Jesus.

Today the children of Brooklyn's ghettos are learning to praise God in the happy, fun atmosphere of Metro.

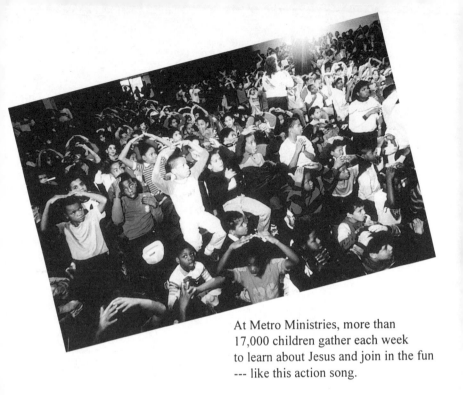

At Metro Ministries, more than
17,000 children gather each week
to learn about Jesus and join in the fun
--- like this action song.

The children of
Metro come to
church on buses like
this one. Special
adult and teen
volunteers called
"Bus Captains" keep
personal tabs on each
of their young charges.

Bill Wilson enjoys a warm and loving rapport with his young congregation.

Each Christmas, friends around the country help provide fully stuffed Christmas stocking for the needy children of Metro. For many it is the only Christmas gift they receive.

Bill Wilson and a member of his
congregation in typical ghetto
settings -- in front of a wall where the
graffiti was recently sprayed-over, and
near one of the many abandoned,
burned-out buildings.

A typical bus-load of Metro Sunday
School children after an exciting day
of learning about Jesus at Metro.

At Metro Sunday School, exciting
action choruses and Bible teaching
are helping the children of Brooklyn
help to follow Jesus.

Bill Wilson and a small dedicated full-time staff -- along with plenty of volunteers -- live and work in the ghetto environment, keeping Metro in shape and reaching out to the children who need the love of Jesus.

The children of Brooklyn's ghettos do not have many options when it comes to lifestyle and future. That's why Metro Ministries is here, offering them Christianity as an alternative lifestyle!

Metro is designed as a haven of happiness and peace
for the children of the ghetto.

Due to the advantage and versatility of a Sidewalk Sunday
School truck, Chris Blake and his team take the gospel to the Bronx.

Chapter 7

Organized Bedlam

Metro Ministries is of little aesthetic value. It has nothing in the way of beauty. It will never be selected as a landmark -- except in the hearts of Christians who witness and appreciate what occurs there.

The outside is pale, beige and flat. Steel doors and locks do not suggest hospitality; but they are an obvious necessity. Inside, the arena-like structure is bright, clean and freshly painted. Rugs cover the floor and movable bleachers stand on either side. The whole center is filled with chairs in regimental order, with one center aisle that divides girls from boys during classes. On the stage is a cross, as well as a life-size wooden cut-out of Yogi Bear, the Sunday School mascot, and various other props.

Through the open doors, children come running, laughing, giggling, skipping in organized bedlam. In a few minutes, the children who have dashed off their buses and passed the high barbed-wire fence outside have filled the church to its 1,000-seat limit, and that's just the junior class. This will be the first of several weekend services. The ancient air conditioner will be taxed to its limit. During New York's bitter winter season, the heating system will roar and groan throughout the proceedings.

The dancing eyes and bright smiles of the mostly minority children bring new meaning to the world "glee." In a world that is harsh and hard, this church is their place of refuge and safety, love and the Lord. When the little band on the side of the stage strikes up the music, the whole congregation jumps to its feet, and -- without a cue -- begins loudly singing and clapping to a lively song. When a slower hymn begins, with the lyrics projected on a screen, gentle melodic sounds fill the air. The children -- often with their arms around each other's waists or shoulders -- sway back and forth in tempo while they sing.

After music, the games start -- silly, funny, frenetic, non-threatening competitions between the boys and the girls. A musical hat game similar to musical chairs, a watermelon-eating contest, and other diversions keep the children roaring with laughter and applause. During a conjuring act, veteran Gospel magician and ventriloquist Bill Wilson (looking like Doug Henning without the fancy duds) leaves his junior audience ooh-ing and aah-ing in surprise as a staff member appears from nowhere in an illusion box - a trick that Bill turns into an illustrated sermon: "Out in the world," he explains, "what you see isn't always what you get. But with Jesus - ah, that's *different.*"

With that, Bill begins a lesson that will last 30 minutes - an eternity for 1,600 kids from the ghettos of Bushwick, Bed-Stuy and Brownsville to sit still. For many of them, discipline is not learned in the home, hardly taught at school, and never practiced on the street. But bedlam turns to boot camp when Bill begins speaking. Monitors roam the aisles to maintain a healthy, alert silence.

Metro's services seem founded upon the words of Lord Byron: "School should be such a joyous place, the penalty for a disruptive child should be that they be forced to leave so that they might appreciate it in the future." A disruptive child receives only one warning in Sunday School; then he's out - and he longs for the moment, not too long away, when he'll be welcomed back in for another chance at mature behavior.

Bill's sermons reveal a multi-media wizardry. There are also tender stories, parables, gentle lectures of God's love for the children ... warnings to resist the immorality of the street scene. Of course, there are no parables of mustard seeds or lilies of the field -- this audience has never seen a lily; they would have trouble relating to such an object lesson.

Bill Wilson is a dynamic and powerful speaker. His voice has a raspish quality - his vocal chords have been worn by much preaching and much of it without a microphone. Yet the sincerity of his heart is a grand substitute for a pretty tone. And his body language expresses the urgency of his message. That urgency brings tears to his eyes... sometimes it reaches his throat and cuts off his words.

The children watch and listen to their pastor; they're surprisingly quiet and attentive. How rarely they have heard words of love and hope -- how rare it is for many of them even to know that someone cares about them! The church contradicts everything they have been taught on the streets -- and sometimes at home. Even during public school recess, teachers shout crude and vile words at them through bullhorns.

The children listen, and before it's all over there is prayer that they will remember and make a commitment that will sustain them. When Bill concludes, the faces of the children shine like Moses, fresh from Mount Sinai.

A theoretical offering is taken. If there is any modern comparison to the story of the widow's mite, it happens here. A dime to these poor little ones might be as much as a hundred-dollar bill to the rest of the world.

Naturally, the children's collection of nickels, dimes and pennies won't be enough to pay for five minutes of electricity to cool the building but there is a lesson here.

As the offering becomes a competition between boys and girls, the children race forward to throw coins into the basket. Some palm their dime or nickel, slide it into their pocket again ... then rush forward 20 seconds later with new resolve to give it all!

Bill's message "gets to them" and it is demonstrated in their heartfelt actions.

Bill Wilson tells the story of the day he glanced into the collection basket and saw a food stamp. Some poor child who didn't have a coin to bring brought the only kind of gift he could think of. Bill can't recall the incident without his eyes gleaming -- and if someone doesn't change the subject, he will have to look away to compose himself.

But all good things, as the saying goes, must come to an end. The children re-board their buses -- it's the same picnic atmosphere that brought them here. Their high spirits stay that way in song -- Marine Corps chants with gospel lyrics joyfully substituted.

The cheerfulness of the drivers, bus captains, volunteers and children alike is a constant surprise. After all, the little ones are to the squalor of the ghettos, the pain of abuse, the darkness of drugs, alcohol and staggering poverty. Still, the children of deprivation are smiling. The ministry of hope to the hopeless is working.

Sidewalk Sunday School was developed here in New York City when the building was filled but there were thousands of kids still out there that no one was reaching. The solution seemed clear. Take Sunday School to them!

Since 1987, the same message taught in Saturday Sunday School reverberates through the streets five days a week as trucks roll throughout the boroughs of New York City and convert into instant Sunday Schools. These Sidewalk Sunday Schools meet at the same time and place every week. "We have 16 trucks with staff and volunteers ministering on sites reaching over 15,000 children weekly.

During the week, there are "Club L.I.F.E." Bible study and recreation meetings for the 1,000 teenagers who have grown up through the Sunday School and have maintained their faith and hope in the transition from childhood to adolescence. They are superb, knowledgeable ministers to their little brothers and sisters. They learn, live and conduct themselves in a Christian manner, despite more grievous temptations than the most grievous nightmares of suburban kids. The Metro ministers and staff work closely with them, guiding, counseling and sharing.

Many of these teenagers will become volunteers, and some perhaps even ministers - if they are not swallowed up in the gutters of the devil.

For some, only Metro Ministries stands between them and that dark oblivion. But it stands strong.

Chapter 8

Reach Out and Touch

WON - BY - ONE

Visitation in the typical evangelical church is often the task relegated to an elderly associate pastor, who calmly makes the hospital rounds and goes home early.

At Metro Ministries, visitation is something entirely different. For Metro's staffers, visitation means running ... and running hard.

The goal is to reach the entire congregation of over 22,000 - mostly poor, mostly living in horrifying dangerous areas, many in families that don't care one way or the other whether their little church member lives or dies.

Where Metro staff and volunteers go daily, violence is a way of life. Every casual visitor is a target. It becomes an important fact to believe that God's power is stronger than switchblades, loaded .38's, drug-crazed addicts and all the other dark aspects of this mission field. Metro staff members and volunteers have to believe in God's protection. They have no other.

The staff and 400 volunteers visit over 20,000 children and families faithfully every week. With nothing but Christian courage, they walk into the crack houses where dealers' children live; the projects and tenement houses where the halls and stairwells reek of defecation and despair. They pick their way through the bodies of addicts strung out on heroin or passed out from alcohol. They come through this minefield of abuse to counsel and encourage parents -- if parents can be found -- and to invite the children to come to church, to come to God, to come beyond the curtain of apathy and horror to a better life ... to Jesus, who can change their hearts.

A policeman would call it a dangerous assignment. A salesman would know he was in hostile territory. A soldier would demand combat pay.

But the Metro soldiers know that their ministry needs constant reinforcement. They must match the devil's work hour-for-hour. They have come to believe this: that in the projects -- where racial hatred and self-destruction are perpetuated -- there are people who need love and self-esteem. To these astonishing spiritual invaders it seems apparent that putting on the armor of God is better than a bulletproof vest. They realize that the people who should be frightening them are really more frightened than they.

Tragically, the ghetto functions like a jungle; the people function like animals. There are more predators than victims; the victims need help, support and the light of the Lord to get them through their hellish existence. It is this concept that drives the volunteers and staff of Metro Ministries.

And they are an effective force. What a surprise and relief it must be for frightened residents behind the multi-locked doors to push them slowly open and see the fresh, bright and smiling faces of those who come in love! What a delight to hear the cheering message: Jesus lives - even in the neglected and dilapidated ghettos ... and God loves even the frightened soul behind the threatening face. These foot soldiers of the Lord's army are brave and resilient. Week after week, Bill Wilson's staff and volunteers brave the elements (postmen have nothing on them) to face the joyless and the hopeless, and to fight in their friendly way for the souls of the little ones.

The visits of Metro staff and volunteers are more than just a simple invitation to church. The children are also carefully looked over for signs of proper nutrition and clothing, and their living conditions are examined for minimum standards. When the kids are in trouble, the Metro leaders are quick to respond with the necessities, often gathered from helpful urban churches or compassionate individuals, or sponsors through the "Won by One" Child Sponsorship program.

There will be no medals for these strange invaders from Metro. Working for the Lord in this corridor of hell provides no material gain, either. The staff receive subsistence support. Yet in their hearts, they know the retirement benefits are eternal.

The children they visit are the bottom line. At Metro Ministries, the bottom line is always the children. They are over 20,000 strong, but they are not statistics. It is one thing to read about the 70,000 kids in this neighborhood alone, growing up below the national poverty level, but it is quite another to meet Laura.

She is nine years old, but she could be six - she is so slight for her age. Dark and smiling, she says she comes to Sunday School because "It's fun ... Jesus is here" But her quizzical expression says she wonders why anyone would ask such a silly question in the first place.

Isa is another of Metro's beautiful children. She's 16, but could be 20; she has the charm and presence of a mature older girl. No charm school gave Isa these qualities. Her mother was a cocaine addict and became a drug dealer before being sent to Riker's Island, a tough New York prison where 70% of women are drug users. By Supreme Court order because of overcrowding, even dangerous criminals are being released early.

Isa and her three-year-old sister found Jesus through the Metro church. She has visited her mother at Riker's Island. Isa's happy report: "Everything will be okay now. I brought Jesus to my mom, and she accepted Him"

Today Isa is a volunteer bus captain.

Juan is a youngster under a cloud. His brother, who had been missing for six months, has finally been found -- dead of an overdose. It's not the first time; another of Juan's brothers overdosed and died last year.

Jenny is an exception to the rule at Metro. The neatly dressed little tyke bounds up the steps to church, a hymn already on her lips. At home her grandmother has dressed her for services and sent her on her way, clapping her hands and laughing. Her mom and dad, who are both working hard for a better life for their family, will be there when Jenny gets out of church.

Ralph is a hostile 10-year-old. He is as illiterate as he is inarticulate, and he attends school only on occasion. He causes fights; he's disruptive...some wonder why he even attends Metro Sunday School week after week. But where else could he find the tough love of the staff member who is now sternly lecturing him after yet another brawl?

Shawn is a serious-looking ten-year-old black child with wide, expressive eyes. He was bagging groceries in a crowded Key Food supermarket when it was held up and the armed robber opened fire on the store management and customers. Shawn was shot through the chest. He is a scarred survivor.

Metro staff members, who had visited Shawn in his home, continued to visit him in the hospital. "Were you afraid?" they asked him about the shooting.

"I went berserk! I was scared!" But through his ordeal Shawn says Jesus helped him feel that everything would be all right. Such is the faith instilled in the children of the Yogi Bear Sunday School.

Shawn is just one of the orphans of the storm who deal with life-threatening violence on a daily basis -- or spend countless hours in rat-infested, cold-water flats, sitting in front of the television, looking at the lifestyles of the rich and famous ... waiting for that welcome knock at the door.

Some of the kids who started attending Metro when the program first began are now grown up, married, and bringing their own children to Sunday School. Although they are dealing with the very real struggles of living in the ghetto, they do their best to be the kinds of moms and dads that they know they need to be - the kind of parents they never had.

Yes, Bill came upon a dead baby in a garbage bag in an empty lot. Yes, he's spent thousands of hours knocking on doors in all kinds of weather over the years. Yes, he's sick and tired of seeing what he sees every day, living here. He's tired of the overwhelming feeling of helplessness.

"'I'll bet I know what motivates you,'" a visitor told him once. "It's the faces of the smiling kids as they get on your bus."

Bill puzzled over whether to laugh or cry or just slap him. Smiling faces don't motivate Bill Wilson. "I think people don't realize, when I knock on a door or pick up a kid in the bus, I'm not just picking up them -- I'm picking up me. Because I was like those little kids once. And when I bend down to help them, I think: maybe out of all this organized bedlam, I can reach another Bill Wilson."

Reaching and building the lives of boys and girls takes extraordinary time and materials. It's not easy, especially surrounded by the violence and poverty of New York City. There is a battle for the lives of these children. So how does the staff organize the monumental task of reaching all these kids one by one?

The answer is WON-BY-ONE.

Metro Ministries' Won-By-One Children's Sponsorship Program provides a direct link between people all over the world who truly care and the children of the inner-city. This active partnership between caring

Christians and children in desperate need has a proven track record of changing lives. In fact, the staff of Metro Ministries sees entire families being rebuilt through the power and work of direct Christian involvement.

Thousands of Christians across the globe, giving $23(US) each month, are providing the resources for effective inner city Christian education and home visits *every week*. Even with the increasing costs of operating a growing ministry in the city, the vast majority of the gifts goes directly to feeding the heart, mind, and soul of every sponsored child. Most importantly, the sponsorships provide each child with the love of a caring Christian. That's because the financial gift is only a part of the involvement. Won-By-One is a rare opportunity for people to continually demonstrate the love of Jesus Christ through prayers and encouragement. With letters and small gifts at Christmas and birthdays, good people everywhere can show a child there is someone, outside the ghetto, who cares about their life.

This makes a bold statement of hope to a child; something they can hold on to. In fact, though the age limit for Won-By-One is 15 years old, many sponsors stay in touch with their child through teen years and beyond.

Bill Wilson will tell you, "It takes time to build a generation. But with a commitment to work together, we can change America . . . One Child At A Time."

For more information concerning Metro Ministries' Won - by-One Child Sponsorship Program, please see the Epilogue after Chapter 10.

Chapter 9

Holy Heroes

The ministry of Metro, from buses to services to visitation, is dependent upon the ministers of Metro. The staff is a heroic lot that deserves a book of its own not just a chapter.

They are white, black, Hispanic. They come as experienced ministers or as novice counselors from every corner of continental America, Hawaii -- even Brooklyn and the Bronx. Bill Wilson has not allowed anyone to join the troupe in innocent ignorance. They all "knew what they were getting into" when they came.

Accommodations are raw at best. Their courage is raw as well. Like new recruits in a military company they have to be taught to survive. They have the armor of Christ in spirit, but learning the ways of the street is of strategic importance as well. Confidence, resignation to the Lord's will, and body language are all equal factors in these risk-filled neighborhoods.

Still, they all seem to agree: "If you don't have anything to die for, you don't have any reason to live."

JoAnn Butler hails from the very un-Brooklyn-like town of Cheraw, South Carolina. "It doesn't matter if you're answering the phone, cleaning toilets, washing or driving a bus," she says sweetly. "It's all for God and the little children." Why did Fausto Lugo leave the best influence in his life? "Why did I ever leave Sunday School? Who cares about me? I have nothing to live for," he said.

These are the thoughts of a desperate 20 year-old incarcerated for over three years. The social pressures in the inner city are intense. The pressure to make big money mixed with the pressure for power and to be "somebody" can be a lethal combination. It took Fausto to Puerto Rico in pursuit of his own "Drug Spot." Soon, with the help of his cousin, he was managing and easily making $500 cash a day. So why flip burgers?

Once back in New York, the thirst for money couldn't be satisfied and he began to mug people. Eventually it all caught up with him and Fausto found that even he couldn't beat the system forever.

Alone and in prison, no money, no friends -- thoughts of God were far from his mind. Survival was the name of the game. Then, a vicious fight landed him five months in solitary confinement. Life was going from bad to worse. When food was served, it was cold and just enough to survive. If he wasn't at the gate to receive it, the guards assumed he didn't want it and skipped him.

Thinking that being out in the yard for recreation would be a good thing, Fausto did all he could to make the list for each day. But one day, he was jumped from behind and his face slashed. He carries the scar to this day and for the rest of his life. That fight cost him another six months in the "box." Sometimes it takes being totally broken before listening and it was no different with Fausto. He was hungry, cut up, lonely and desperate.

Silently, he was making plans to end it all when an officer came to his cell. The officer gave him a bag containing his personal property kept at another prison. As Fausto dejectedly emptied the bag, out tumbled his Bible. He started to cry. This hard, tough, broken young man began to remember the years of going to Sunday School. He remembered going to *Club L.I.F.E.* as a youth. He couldn't help but recall what he'd been taught. "I yearned for the time when I was standing with God."

Hungrily, he read his Bible and prayed for the first time in years. "I felt the Lord's presence in the cell with me. I asked Him to free me. My prison wasn't just physical, it was spiritual, too. God met me that night and I was set free!"

It took only seven months for him to be released from

prison. Fausto went back to Metro and worked as a janitor just to be close and to give back to God anything he could. In time his desire to minister grew and he now serves full-time and preaches at Sidewalk Sunday School. "I know God has a calling on my life to minister to teenagers and kids. Whenever I can, I tell them about the love of Jesus Christ. I tell them that even though I was a criminal, cut people, stabbed people and sold drugs, I was set free. Jail didn't rehabilitate me, Jesus Christ changed my direction."

And who pointed Fausto to Jesus Christ? His Bus Captain. His youth pastors. The little lady who gave out of her grocery money. Folks who support this ministry.

The Won-by-One Sponsorship Program of Metro Ministries is becoming more important to the ministry and to the children it serves each day. Fortunately, God delivered an incredible woman to direct this huge project - a task of true love.

Her name is Esther Ramsaroop.

Esther came to the United States with her family from Guyana over ten years ago. Her parents felt that life in the U.S. would be better for their younger son who had been tragically disabled due to an accident.

Soon she looked for a church where her energy and zeal could be utilized. A friend told her about Metro and after her first visit, she never left.

As a yielded vessel, perhaps it's the constant care Esther's brother needs; or her strong ministerial background; or the struggle she recently endured as a devastating fire destroyed her home that have all nurtured the strong compassion she pours out for so many children and their families.

For seven years, Esther commuted from Manhattan to Brooklyn at least twice a week, visited kids, worked in Sunday School all day and took a bus to her home in Queens. Life was full and interesting.

Meanwhile, she was climbing up the corporate ladder quite quickly. Soon Esther found herself at a crossroads in Manhattan. Change was in the air and she began to look around. Two competing companies continued offering higher and higher salaries. But, peace would not come. All the while, she was volunteering at Metro. Wisely, she went away to seek the Lord.

Contrary to human wisdom, she began working at Metro within a month for little or nothing of what the Manhattan companies offered. Six months later she became the Department head of the ever-growing Won-by-One Sponsorship Program.

Today she knows at least three-quarters of the sponsored kids by name, the area they live in and who their Bus Captain is without "checking her records."

She knows many of the sponsors by voice and name. She's amazing. But more than her remarkable ability to recall so many people, is her strength of leadership and compassion.

She runs a tight ship which is a good thing since Won-by-One's influence is continuing to expand with the sponsorship age being raised to 15 years old. These faithful youths are often the workers within Sunday School itself.

Esther's continuing goal for the Won-by-One department is for greater and improved communications between child, sponsor and the ministry. Without hesitancy, she believes this ministry is for the kids and for eternity.

She takes this responsibility very seriously. In fact, she's been known to cry over the kids. Esther often says, "I know the sponsors care as much about the kids as we do because they give us the tools to reach out to the kids and their families. That really makes a difference. Sometimes the difference isn't seen immediately. But, I've seen their love bear fruit years after the child has grown into adulthood." If you're not yet a sponsor, why not call Esther and reach one more before it's too late?

The rest of the Metro staff and volunteers - too many to mention here - consider themselves equally rich, simply because they are able to do God's will.

"God sends the right people at the right time," Wilson believes. "He always has and He always will."

It's a staff like this that allows Bill to travel to raise funds, secure that things are carrying on as they should, and to know that God's hand is directing the ministry through this talented staff, because without them there would be no ministry here in Brooklyn.

On a daily basis, they deal with filth, burnout, fear, ingratitude and even despair. It would be easy to walk away. But they don't.

Thank God for that. Thank God for them.

Chapter 10

Running on Empty

To know Bill Wilson is to comprehend the loneliness of the long-distance runner. He has given so much of himself that there is little left for his own life. Many of the youngsters in his unusual congregation call him Bill ... or Dad. He is loved and respected by his staff, and has earned the love and respect of ministers and congregations nationally -- even of those who have never met him. Yet when it comes to bearing the burden for his ministry, Bill stands alone.

And he doesn't know how to say no. He firmly denies the fact that there are only 24 hours in a day. He rarely walks; he runs. But he never seems to go dry. Even when he's running on empty, he keeps running.

His schedule is self-imposed and merciless. The fatigue in his eyes is reflected in his whole body. He has missed more meals than most people his age have eaten.

On weekends, the day begins as early as 5:30. On Father's Day, for instance, Metro invited the parents of their little parishioners and the occupants of a local men's shelter to join them for services and a picnic lunch. Bill was up early -- preparing, watching the morning dawn grey. The weatherman predicted rain, but Bill was optimistic that the picnic would go on outdoors as scheduled.

The skies stayed glowering and black; but after the church service, each member carried a chair to a parking lot a block away, where the picnic tables had been set up. The wonderful smells of food and hospitality -- uncommon treasures in Bushwick -- filled the air. The children were delighted, the parents surprised, and the men from the shelter amazed as the loving generosity poured out. Metro staff members ran from grill to table and back again, making sure that everyone was happy, well-fed and satisfied.

Gospel singers filled the air with sacred music; then Bill Wilson mounted a makeshift stage, built on the side of a van, to preach and teach with fire. No rendering of platitudes, but a hard-nosed and real sermon, as mean and true as the streets of Brooklyn. The people in the tenement houses surrounding the lot leaned out their windows to hear, and the street people across the way lowered the bottles from their lips to listen.

When the sermon was done, 24 people came forward to make a commitment to Jesus. For them, life began all over again this Father's Day. The sky was still grim and threatening, but not a drop of rain fell.

Although weekends are busy for Bill Wilson, weekdays are no less jam-packed. They start with a staff meeting at 8:30 sharp, then an hour or two to plan a fun-filled but effective illustration of God's presence in the lives of children. Then there are plans to be laid for Club L.I.F.E. -- how to help teenagers combat the corruption of the streets.

Then Bill has to write pastors and donors who have been so generous - he is always swimming upstream, it seems, to keep the ministry afloat financially. Plus, he must greet and situate the latest work crew from California, Ohio, Canada, Europe or Asia who are spending their vacations gutting an abandoned home for new staff housing or fixing the electrical system in the old pretzel factory.

Afterward he's got to straighten out this problem with the city -- they're after the ministry for not having an elevator inspected, even though it's been sealed off, unused, for 15 years. Then Bill will make time for a staff member who is discouraged -- maybe on the verge of burnout.

Ten phone messages go unanswered on his desk. He must get to at least five of them, but he will rely on the charity of the others he doesn't have time to answer.

Then there's study time and prayer time and time to console the afflicted -- a child whose father was murdered last week. Later Bill will race to catch a plane to Orlando, Tulsa, Phoenix, Holland or Malaysia ... wherever he will be sharing his mission tonight, and asking for the prayers and support of Christian friends.

On the way out the door to the airport, he gives his support staff 15 assignments and promises to be back in time to visit the children on his regular route and drive his bus on Saturday, hold a meeting with the staff and some new volunteers, see that the flyers are ready, come up with an exciting teaching gimmick for the service -- and get out a newsletter.

On the way to the airport -- during the commonplace hour-long delay before boarding -- and on the long flight to another engagement, the loneliness sets in. After many such long journeys, every modest hotel room looks the same, and another polite congregation waits to hear the incredible tale...

But every time, the comfortable middle-class Christians get more than they bargained for as Bill opens his heart, sharing the frightening and beautiful story of his Sunday School in no man's land.

This year, Bill Wilson will travel 250,000 miles preaching, teaching and asking for support and prayers for his mission. In just a few months, he'll travel further than the Apostle Paul on a lifetime of missionary journeys. But the shared message of Paul the Apostle and Bill Wilson - "Jesus Christ and Him crucified" -- will keep Bill motivated ... and moving forward until journey's end.

Bill Wilson gets grumpy -- "touchy" might be a better word -- when people equate him personally to Metro. The ministry, he claims, is not Bill Wilson. He sees, all too clearly, the crucial role of his hard-driven staff, of the devoted volunteers, of the loyal but invisible donors and prayer-warriors. He knows that they are Metro ... and Bill Wilson is only the catalyst.

But God -- in His inexplicable wisdom -- works through men ... individuals ... planting visions in their hearts and harvesting miracles in maddening mission fields like Bushwick.

Bill Wilson, in spite of aching fatigue, crushing discouragement, horrifying obstacles ... stands true to that calling.

Not for recognition, not for glory. For the children.

And for Jesus, as he quotes from a Gospel song: "He paid a debt He did not owe; I owe a debt I cannot pay." But, Bill Wilson adds, "I'll die trying."

Epilogue

You are the Rest of the Story

Now you can help Metro Ministries save one child at a time.

Metro Ministries' Won-By-One Children's Sponsorship Program is changing the lives of children and their families every day.

But, this will not continue to happen without you.

Will you help one child? That's the key question. Because the **Won-By-One** program allows you to bring an enormous benefit to the life of *one very special child.* Just $23 (US) each month gives them effective Christian education and home visits *every week.* You know that since 1980, Bill Wilson and Metro Ministries have helped to pioneer ministries in the forgotten inner-cities of America. Their mission is to find and rescue the children left behind in this battleground of drugs, violence, abuse, and filth.

By throwing out the old rule books, Bill began several effective children's ministry programs that had to work in the chaos of the inner-city. This was a struggle that could only be won with the power of God. Through the years enormous with faith and persistence Bill began Sunday Schools, new churches and the **Won-By-One Children's Sponsorship Program.**

"It's easier to build boys and girls than to repair men and women," Bill Wilson often says. Building the lives of boys and girls takes extraordinary time and materials. It's not easy, especially surrounded by the violence and poverty of New York City. There is a battle for the lives of these children.

Please consider the challenge . . . and the hope. There are millions of children in need and in danger. Be honest, ask yourself, "How long can they wait?"

The answer is in your hands.

You have the opportunity right now to bring them hope. By the help and grace of God, the lives of thousands of children are changed each year through your love. You can fight the city and win! Help save these children by supporting of the **Won-By-One** program of Metro Ministries.

The children are waiting.

Please fill out this form and return it to Metro Ministries today: **P.O. Box 695, Brooklyn, NY 11237**
Or contact us: www.metroministries.org

Bill:
I want to be a part of Metro Ministries' **Won-by-One**
Sponsorship Program!
I'm enclosing $_____ in order to sponsor:
  ❑ A child. ($23US per month)
  ❑ Children:
  _____ Number of Children you want to sponsor. ($23US per month for each child sponsored)
I would like to sponsor:
  ❑ A girl
  ❑ A boy
  ❑ Either

Your Name: _____

Street Address _____

City _____   State _____

Zip\Postal Code_____   Country _____

E_mail_____

For more information please contact Metro Ministries
directly at:
Phone: 718-453-3352
Fax: 718-453-7177
www.metroministries.org

The children are waiting.